Finger Painting Praise

The poems in *Fingerpainting with Words*
are succinct and expansive. They open out
and take a reader in. They liberate a reader
in the poet's real and imaginary world. To
read them is to be exhilarated and refreshed.
Striking in their originality of sight, sense,
and sound, to read them is to know what it
means to be human, to be delightfully
surprised, cognizant of the idea that we think
by feeling.

Peter Mladinic, author of *Knives on a Table*

Who is Nolcha Fox?

- The poet whose Fingerpainting with Words includes twenty-four works previously printed in seven literary magazines...
- The daughter and wife, spinning amazing poetic imagery of mother, husband, cold coffee, and burnt dinners...
- The magician exploring dead letters and that other place on the other side of this instant...
- The alchemist, turning water, sun, and sky into sunburned skins and plastic smiles...
- My friend, who asked me to write something about *Fingerpainting with Words*—so here it is, Nolcha dear, because that's what friends are for.

Maxim W, Furek, author of *The Flying Saucer Esoteric: History's Most Amazing UFO Events*

Fingerpainting with Words

by Nolcha Fox

Garden of Neuro Publishing
A Division of the Garden of Neuro Institute
Poughkeepsie, New York
www.GardenofNeuroPublishing.com
Copyright © Nolcha Fox 2024

ISBN NUMBER 979-8-9851332-8-8
Cover Design by: Nanci Arvizu

Acknowledgments

Thanks to Alexander Grey for his cover art from Unsplash.

Thanks to these literary magazines that published my poems:

- *Alien Buddha Zine*: "Fragrance"
- *Contemplate*: "Secondhand"
- *Garden of Neuro*: "Ripening," "Thirsty"
- *iPoetry*: "Catch Them," "Why I Can't Write This Poem"
- *Medium*: "The Sky Is a Lie"
- *Medusa's Kitchen*: "a bridge of," "Beached," "Through a Bus Window," "Thumbing a Ride," "Vacancy"
- *Muddyum*: "Lunch"

Thanks to my mother, who loved me before I was born. She always applauded everything I wrote.

A special thanks to my husband, whom I love dearly. He's held my hand for the past 24 years so that I won't fly away.

Table of Contents

Finger Painting With Words

A bridge of

braided hair and bone,
placenta plundered,
mothered, daughtered,
umbilical umbrellaed,
connecting us through time
and space.

An Instant

This instant is divided by curtains of
water
and the sound of shuddering time.
Cup this instant between your palms,
make it a prayer.
Open your hands, this instant flies to
the heavens.
Hold this instant in your mouth, it is
water between your teeth.
This instant is your footsteps parting
the grass,
this instant is the wind rippling the
grass,
and the name of these grasses in this
wind
is that other place on the other side
of this instant.

First and last lines from "The Name
of that Silence is These Grasses in
the Wind" by JJJJJerome Ellis

Another Dead Letter

Not what's lost
in some locked room
in envelopes
undelivered,
no, it's the letters
that fail to form
into words, dropping
from my lips,
dead weights,
dead letters,
an embarrassment
of failed
migrations.

Beached

The summer beats on
sunburned skins
so tightly packed together.
We're one beached whale,
gasping sun and longing
for the water.

Catch Them

In morning dark, the stars are
blinding white,
rampaging fireflies on steroids.
Hollyhocks defy gravity and aphids
to kiss the sky before the weight of
summer
tilts them to kiss the ground.
Heat bakes the sidewalk
into squares of peanut butter fudge,
sweet sludge from oven top.
Each second a butterfly
I scoop with net of tangled words
before it flies pastward to cocoon.

Clouds form

an empty snakeskin
in shades of grey and gold
that hiss and slither
above me to a place
I will not go

Fragrance

The wind opens
the cafe door,
waltzes in with
night blooming jasmine,
dressed in
pink-drenched clouds.
She stirs a latte
with a fingertip
painted purple lilacs.
Streetlights pull
up a chair
next to the window,
and wink through
fragrant listening.

Happiness is a tree

growing in the kitchen, watered
with tears and cold coffee.
It grows in silence. breathing in
burnt dinners and collapsed cakes.
Its branches grow high
in open-window breeze
and early morning sunrise.
Its roots dig deep through
sleepless nights and bad choices.
So familiar a tree, we walk
right through it, forgetting
we planted it, we own it.

I Don't Know Where They Go

The sweet breeze whirls clouds
aflutter, silk scarves I'll never wear.
Flowers bloom before I wake,
petals lost before I sleep.
Chokecherries bend branches,
a weight too sour for sugar
decaying on the grass.
I barely blink, the world transformed
to what I cannot grasp.

Lunch

Soggy, squishy, limp,
a brick I dragged
in paper bag to school.
It waited in the heat
of day, little chickees
screeching mayonnaise
and rotting between bread.
Lunchtime groan
I unwrapped death
that wrapped me in
a cloud of noxious fumes.
The other kids left me
alone to croak from
chicken salad sandwich.

Noon

Noon is a wreck of sunlight
afloat on receding shadows

Noon is a bald sweat
glistening on rose petals.

Noon is a disco dance
on a burner set to high.

Noon is a memory of flying
in the eyelids of dusk.

Ripening

A vague, fuzzy fruit,
past ripening,
wrinkled, blemished,
my brilliance dimmed,
my tartness sweetened,
I'm calmer now,
decomposing, composting,
relishing the fading
glow of sunset.

Secondhand

He grumbled that the sunrise woke
him up
and now he couldn't fall asleep.
He sloshed his coffee, slammed the
door,
and stumbled off to work.
I found the sunrise lounging on the
bed,
awash in crayon colors, morning
breeze
and robin song.
I stuffed sunrise in my mouth.
I tasted dew-swept grass and flower
petals
baked in bread that rose to greet the
day.
I reused the sunrise that my husband
tossed aside.

Someday I'll Be in Love with Light

In the aftermath of consolation,
when casseroles and cakes
from friends and family disappear,
they leave a house empty of your
laugh,
your shadow missing from the walls.
Black coffee is a cup of anticipation
of sun warming the hollow of your
chair,
of rain-jeweled flowers in the vase,
a parting of waterfalls of mourning.

Static Electricity

Sunset is spark
and crackle,
pink and orange
lightning, as day
puts on her woolen suit
to greet the coolness
of the night

Stoic Oak

Lives scurry, hurry past the oak.
No notice of the limbs that stroke the
stars,
how bark erases teenage pen-knifed
hearts.
Unseen roots lap up the thirsty hours
of light.
Leaves shade secret rendezvous.
Out of sight, this oak holds
sky and earth in place.

The Sky Is a Lie

The clouds dim to charcoal,
bullies puffing their chests
flexing their muscles.
The sun sees fear under the bravado,
scattering the clouds
and revealing the lie of rain.

Thirsty

I'm a cool glass of water
flowing down the street
in clingy clothes
that ripple as I walk.
Behind me streams
a panting parade,
longing for a drink.

Through a Bus Window

I shiver in my shirt
full of black holes
that whisper despair
and come hither,
as the sun sets over
a herd of rusted trailers
galloping backward
out of view.
This road is a ribbon of white
dipped in cloudburst
and melting into a future
I can't see.

Thumbing a Ride

She stands on a dark country road,
thumb out, looking for a ride.
I've seen her fractured face
at the bottom of a bottle,
in the needle tracks to
the edge of a cliff.
Her leather jacket stinks
of burnt rubber racing
across the railroad tracks.

This is one hitchhiker to hell
I don't pick up.

Vacancy

Your eyes divine
shine vacancy,
you wilt under
under my stare.
You curl into
an ampersand,
unroll into
a question mark.
You are a feather
in my throat
that unravels
into a bird.

Veiled

We wear veils to the wedding,
faces faded under lace.
Out of photos, out of focus,
we take our designated place.
This moment must be perfect,
we flash face-paint plastic smiles.
We retire to private hells
where we unveil imperfections
dipped in cheap champagne.

What He Gets

He gives her flowers.
She is a geyser,
shucking his skin.

He gives her chocolates.
She is a flash flood of tears,
a whirlpool that drowns him.

He would say goodbye,
but he is already gone.

Why I Can't Write This Poem

Words are the skirts
that swirl out the door
with a hint of White Shoulders.

Words are a breath
I hold for a moment
before it flies free.

Words are ice crystals
that melt in the air
into raindrops.

Words are….
oh, never mind.
I forgot what I wanted to write.

About the Author

Nolcha Fox's poems have been curated in print and online journals. Her poetry books are available on Amazon and Dancing Girl Press. Nominee for 2023 Best of The Net, 2024 Best of the Net Anthology. Nominee for a 2023 Pushcart Prize. Editor for Garden of Neuro. Visual editor for Chewers & Masticadores.

Garden of Neuro Institute Poet Laureate 2024

Books by Nolcha Fox

Website: https://bit.ly/3bT9tYu
"My Father's Ghost Hates Cats"
https://amzn.to/3uEKAqa
"The Big Unda" https://amzn.to/3IxmJhY
"How to Get Me Up in the Morning"
https://amzn.to/3RLDaKc
"Memory is that raccoon"
https://www.amazon.com/dp/9395224622/
"Cow Candy"
https://www.amazon.com/Cow-Candy-
Nolcha-Fox/dp/9395224789/
"Why Chicken Explodes in the Microwave"
https://dulcetshop.myshopify.com/products/
why-chicken-explodes-in-the-microwave-
nolcha-fox

Connect with Nolcha Fox

Facebook: nolcha.fox
Twitter: @FoxNolcha
Medium: @nolchafox_14571

Garden of Neuro Pubishing is a Division of
The Garden of Neuro Institute

www.GardenofNeuro.org

www.GardenofNeuroPublishing.com

Call for Submissions for women and
gender+ projects.

Authors are invited to submit manuscripts
for publishing consideration.